The Sherman at War

(2) The US Army in the European Theater 1943-45

Text and color plates by Steven Zaloga

We welcome authors who can help

expand our range of books. If you

would like to submit material,

please feel free to contact us.

We are always on the look-out for new,

unpublished photos for this series.

If you have photos or slides or

information you feel may be useful to

future volumes, please send them to us

for possible future publication.

Full photo credits will be given upon

publication.

ISBN 962-361-669-4

printed in Hong Kong

Introduction

This book follows an earlier one in the "Armor at War" (
7001) series published in 1994. This book consists of a new se
of photos of the M4 Sherman in combat with the US Army in
European Theater during World War II. The M4 Sherman was
most widely used US tank of the war, with more Sherm
manufactured than all German tanks combined. This book provi
more detailed coverage of some of the campaigns than the previ
volume, especially new coverage of the tank fighting in Italy
1944-45, and more in-depth coverage of the fighting along
German Siegfried line in the autumn and winter of 1944-45.
author has discovered a large number of new, previou
unpublished photos of the M4 in combat. These photos includ
series of photos of tanks of the US Ninth Army that were
released to the public and which remained buried in the archi
until recently. It also includes a number of rare photos from priv
collections. Unless otherwise noted, these photos are all official
Army Signal Corps or US Navy photos. The author would like
thank the archivists who have helped in locating these pho
including Charles Lemons at the Patton Museum, Ft. Knox; Rar
Hackenburg, at Special Collections, US Army Military Hist
Institute, Carlisle Barracks; and Alan Aimone, at Spec
Collections, US Military Academy, West Point.

The M4A1 medium tank was first deployed with the British 8th Army in h Africa in 1942. This is a rare view of the fifth production tank, tration number T-25193 named "Link", in a workshop in Egypt having its -shields fitted before being issue to troops. It is still fitted with the short 5mm gun with counter-weights. In British service, the M4 was named herman after the Civil War general, but this name was seldom used by JS Army during the war. (Jarrett collection, MHI Archives)

A rear view of a M4A1 from 1st Arm'd Regt. knocked out at Sidi bou Zid. The tank has sunken into the soft soil, a problem that would plague to M4 in service due to its narrow track.

The combat debut of the M4A1 with American troops was not icious. This is a M4A1 of the 1st Arm'd. Regt., 1st Armored Div. which knocked out in fighting with the Afrika Korps at Sidi bou Zid on 14-15 uary 1943 during the German counter-attack through the Kasserine . The heavy losses of M4 tanks in these engagements had more to do inexperience than with any technical problems with the tank.

The battlefield around Sidi bou Zid is ed with burned out M4A1 tanks of the Arm'd Regt. The tank in the foreground completely burned out, and as a result turret markings appear darker. These 1 are early production types evident the hinged driver's visors and the early 893 vertical volute suspension.

Although the 1st Armored Regiment was largely equipped with the [cast] hull M4A1, it also had the M4 with welded hull as seen here, a tank from [Co.] F, 1st Arm'd Regt. knocked out during the 15 February counterattac[k by] Combat Command C southwest of Sidi Salem. This tank was knocke[d out] by a 5cm round from a German Pz.Kpfw III tank. These are early produ[ction] M4 tanks with the early suspension, early pattern armored visors fo[r the] driver and co-driver, and the early gun mantlet without the armored co[llar.]

A M4A1 from 1st Arm'd Regt. knocked out near Tell el Aggagir. This tank has taken several hits and is completely burned out after having suffered an internal ammunition fire. There is a common myth that the Sherman's propensity to fire was due to its gasoline engine. In fact, ammunition fires were the main threat.

The losses suffered during the Kasserine Pass disaster were replaced by new supplies. This M4A1 has just arrived at Oran in North Africa on 5 [March] 1943. Unlike the M4A1 tanks lost at Kasserine Pass, it is the newer version with the improved D47527 suspension, and the revised hull casting with driv[er] periscopes replacing the hinged view slits.

The 1st Armored Division was not the only US tank unit in Tunisia. Here, a M4A1 of Co. A, 751st Tank Battalion moves down a street in Bizerte following their entry into the city on 7 May 1943. The capture of Bizerte and the surrounding area marked the end of the North African campaign. (Patton Museum)

The Scorpion detonated mines by "flailing" them with [heav]y chains. Although the provision of 100 of these was [requ]ested by the European Theater HQ, the Ordnance [Dept.] instead decided to supply US Army units with roller-mine exploders for operations in Europe.

North Africa served as a staging area for US Army operations in the Mediterranean. Here, an ordnance unit is examining a Scorpion flail tank provided [by t]he British 8th Army. The British army had undertaken development of flail tanks for rapid breaching of mine-fields and had first used them in North Africa.

For Operation "Husky", the amphibious assault on Sicily, the 2nd Armored Division provided the armored shock force of Patton's Seventh Army. Here, a M4A1 moves down a street in Gela on 11 July 1943, site of one of the American landings. Tank fighting on Sicily was limited in scope, in no small measure due to the inept leadership of the Herman Göring Panzer Division.

A 2nd Armored Division M4 on an overpass near Mistretta, Sicily c[?] August 1943, three weeks after the area had been captured. Sicily saw[?] first use of the "Allied star" insignia, a white star in a white circle, introd[?] after North Africa to prevent the star from being mistaken for a German c[?] at a distance.

The Sicily landings were followed by landings in Italy proper with the assault at Salerno on 9 September 1943. Armored support in the American se[?] was provided by the 751st Tank Battalion and the 191st Tank Battalion. The water off the Paestum beach was too shallow for LSTs, forcing the navy to de[?] pontoon ramps to get the tanks ashore like these M4A1 tanks.

This M4A1 named "Bull O' The Woods" is being recovered after sliding [of]f a road. It is camouflage painted in the earth yellow/olive drab scheme [esta]blished for the Sicily landings. The tank carries its tactical number, "1*6" [on t]he turret rear separated by the star, a pattern common in Fifth Army tank [unit]s.

Fighting in Italy in early 1944 focused around the German Gustav line defenses near Cassino. Here a signals lineman attempts to clean up telephone lines that have been draped on an overturned M4 medium tank knocked out in the fighting near Cassino in January 1944.

A M4 from Co. C, 756th Tank Battalion lies abandoned in a water[log]ged ditch during the fighting along the Rapido river on 8 February 1944. [Thi]s unit proved valuable in providing close-support for infantry units during [the] late January fighting on the approaches to Cassino.

A M4 tank, "B-9" from Co. B, 756th Tank Battalion, knocked out in the approaches to Cassino by two direct hits on the transmission housing in early February 1944. Engineers are checking the bridge abutment for mines.

This M4 has suffered an internal [am]munition fire which has burned it out [com]pletely and blown the lower [gla]nson panel downward on to the [trac]ks. An engineer is attempting to [rea]ttach the tracks so that the tank can [be] cleared from the road.

A pair of M4A1 tanks knocked while supporting the Fre Expeditionary Corps' attack on M Belvedere in late January 1944. H some troops from the US Army Mountain Division explore the wre while passing through on 20 Febru 1944.

Operations in the mountainous Italian conditions convinced the US Army of the need for more engineer support of tank units. Here, the 16th Engineer Battalion conducts trials of a treadway bridge for crossing anti-tank ditches and other obstructions, using a M4A1 medium tank named "One Fault".

After months of frustration and stalema in May 1944, the US Fifth Army began a ma offensive against the Gustav line in conjunc with the neighboring British Eight Army. 88th Infantry Division struck from Castelfo supported by M4 tanks of the 760th Ta Battalion. The tank in the foreground has barely legible cartoon painted on the side, "B of Little Rock".

This M4 of the 760th Tank Battalion took [part?] in the fighting on Monte SS Cosma [e Damiano?] [Dam]iano on 13 May 1944 during the 88th [Infantry?] [Infant]ry Division attack. By this stage of the [camp]aign, the tanks were painting out the Allied [recog]nition star as it presented too clear a [target?] for German anti-tank gunners.

Mines were one of the primary menace's to tanks in the Italian theater, accounting for about a quarter of all tank losses in Italy. This M4 of the 755th Tank Battalion near Castelforte has had its lead bogie assembly completely blown off. This is one of the newer M4 tanks, with additional applique armor added in front of the driver's stations and on the right side of the turret front.

[To] the right of the American [ass]ault, Gen. Juin's French [Exp]editionary Force launched an attack [on t]he German 71st Infantry Division in [the] Monte Majo area. Here, on 13 May [194]4, a French M6 37mm gun motor [car]riage and jeep pass by a M4 [me]dium tank of the 755th Tank [Bat]talion knocked out earlier in the [figh]ting.

Following the penetration and collap the Gustav line in mid-May 1944 an capture of Monte Cassino, the Allied force moved on to the so-called Hitler line approaches to Rome. Among the formidable defenses in the Hitler line Panther tank turrets emplaced as defenses covering key road junctions. tanks of the 760th Tank Battalion move p tank knocked out in fighting earlier on 14 1944 along the Minturno-Santa Maria In road while supporting the attack by the Infantry Regiment. The M4A1 to the probably one of the tanks of Co. C led Gleisner that were knocked out on the mo of 12 May 1944 to Teller mines.

During the fighting in the Mt. Bracchi hills, the 760th Tank Battalion supported the 351st Infantry in the capture of Formia on 14 May 1944. This is a view of M4A1 tanks of Co. A and B, 760th Tank Battalion line along the streets of Formia on 15 May 1944 after the town was captured.

A close-up of one of the tanks of Co. B, 760th T Battalion in Formia. The shipping marking can be s on the engine doors, a common form of unit markin the Italian theater.

Mine's could set off internal ammunition stowage with horrific results as ⁄n by this M4 blown open during fighting near Borgo Sabotino on 23 1944.

In hopes of circumventing the stalemate along the Gustav line, in January 1944 the US VI Corps landed at Anzio, south of Rome. Instead of relieving the Allied forces, the Anzio force became trapped in the lodgement until May 1944. With the renewal of the Allied offensive against Cassino in May 1944, the forces at Anzio prepared to break-out for Rome, codenamed "Operation Buffalo". Leading the attack was the 1st Armored Division. This is an M10 tank destroyer of the division's 710th Tank Destroyer Bn. knocked out alongside a M4 tank named "Fighting Gator" during the savage fighting along the Cisterna road on 22 May 1944.

One of the more novel concepts attempted in the Anzio break-out was the "Battle Sled" idea pioneered by the commander of the 3rd Division, Gen. J.W. ⁄n Mike" O'Daniel. These metal sleds were designed to be towed behind tanks to attack heavily protected objectives. This is a training exercise on 10 June ⁄4.

Numerous tanks were lost by the [?] Armored Division along the Velletri-Cis[?] highway during the May 1944 fighting. [?] M4A1 and M4 were still left alongside the [?] a year later in May 1945 when this phot[?] taken.

GIs from the 6th Armored Infantry Regiment pass by a destroyed M4 tank of the 1st Armored Division that has suffered from a catastrophic internal ammunition explosion during the fighting along the Cisterna highway on 22 May 1944. The tank was a victim of a landmine, and white engineer tape strung along the road is intended to keep troops from wandering into the minefield.

This M4A1 of the 1st Armo[?] Division is winched on to a ta[?] transporter after being knocked [?] during "Operation Buffalo". The turre[?] pock-marked with many small cal[?] hits which have failed to penetrate [?] armor. As will be noticed, the [?] Armored Division was still opera[?] many early production M4A1 tanks [?] this time without the added glacis, [?] or turret applique armor.

Rome finally fell to the Allies on 4 June 1944, and the pursuit of the Germans soon followed. This is a M4 operating north of the city on 10 June 1944. is an early production M4 with the hinged driver's view slits.

No sooner had the Fifth Army captured Rome, but that significant ions of its forces were taken away to assist in the forthcoming operations France. The Seventh Army began forming along the Italian coast to ich an amphibious invasion, codenamed Operation "Dragoon", against thern France. This is a harbor in Italy on 31 July 1944 with forces ssing for the landing. The M4 tanks in the foreground have been pared for the landing by being water-proofed and wading trunks added. ice that the turret ring and other openings have been covered by abination of canvas and mastic sealant.

A column of M4A1 tanks move along the coast near Bagnoli, Italy on 10 just 1944 in preparations for the landings in southern France later in the k. The lead tank has its deep wading trunks fitted, and canvas and stic sealant have been applied to the gun mantlet and turret ring.

An M4A1 tank of the 1st Arm'd Regt., 1st Arm
Division, knocked out by a hit from the rear
penetrated the center of the turret ring. The resu
ammunition fire has blown the turret off the tank.

The 1st Armored Division remained in Italy
Fifth Army even though a number of the Fifth Ar
separate tank battalions were transferred to Sev
Army in southern France. Here, the crew of a M4A
Co. B, 13th Arm'd. Regt. take a breather in the
country north of Rome in the summer of 1944. Ca
inspection of the turret front shows the attachment c
improvised artillery sight over the gunner's sight.
was relatively common in the division since it was o
used to provide indirect artillery fire support. (Pa
Museum)

A M4A1 tank of 1st Armo
Division moves through the town
Ponsacco on 1 September 1944 du
the initial phases of the offens
against the Gothic line. Two strips
T49 metal grouser track have be
attached to the glacis plate to provid
measure of added armor protection.

A T2 recovery vehicle prepares to recover a burned out M4A3 (76) hit by German artillery fire during the fighting along the Gothic Line. German artillery fire in the area was intense, including 28cm guns. The T2, later designated as the M31, was the standard US armored recovery vehicle during the war, and was based on the old M3 medium tank chassis.

A M4 tank of the 752nd Tank Battalion passes a column of trucks and near San Piero on 13 September 1944, a day after the start of the II offensive against the German Gothic Line north of Florence.

A close up of the knocked out M4A3 (76) shows that fire has burned the rubber off the tracks and suspension on the right side of the tank. The 1st ored Division began receiving the uparmed M4 with 76mm gun in the late summer of 1944.

M4 tanks of the 755th Tank Battalion are us[] provide indirect artillery fire support during the sa[] fighting on Monte Battaglia on 1 October 1944. [] nearest vehicle, "A7", has had an improvised f[] added to engine deck to help carry crew stowage [] ammunition.

During mid-October, the 751st Tank Batta[] supported Task Force 92's attack towards the Go[] line near Massa. This is a M4A1 from the unit's Co[] This is from an early production batch with the e[] style of mantlet with no armored cheeks on the sid[] the gun tube.

16

A close-up view of one of the tanks o. A, 755th Tank alion while ucting fire support ations from the near Pietramala 1 October 1944. has been tied g the hull side to h natural foliage uflage.

A M4A1 of the 752nd Tank Battalion gives an assist to a M18 76mm gun motor carriage of the 701st Tank Destroyer Battalion that has become bogged n on a hill on 11 December 1944. Behind these vehicles are a T2 armored recovery vehicle and a pair of M4 tanks, including one of the newer ones with m gun.

An overhead view of the M4A1 from 752nd Tank Batt
towing the M18. Another M18 can be seen bogged down i
field behind.

"Cozy II", a M4 of Co. C, 751st Tank Battalion fires on targets near Belvedere, Italy on 22 February 1945. The solider on the right is observing the fire away from the tank, as often the smoke from the tank gun and machine guns would obscure the target to the tank crew.

One of the multiple rocket launchers used in Italy was the 7.2 inch M17 "Whizbang". It was used in relatively modest numbers, and a few were sent to southern France with Seventh Army.

M4A1 "C-9", named "Comic", of Co. C, 751st Tank Battalio
operations near Mt. Valbura, Italy on 14 April 1945. Besides the bur
code identifying the unit, the tank also has its shipping code, "6692", pai
below and to the left.

The landings in Normandy on 6 June 1944 were supported by M4 tanks
e Duplex Drive (DD) configuration, and tanks with deep wading trunks.
tank, "H2 Hurricane" from Co. H, 66th Armored Regt., 2nd Armored Div.
es ashore at Utah beach on D+1. The wading trunks were added to
y tanks since the LSTs could often not make it all the way to the beach.
wading trunks allowed the tank to be dropped in water deeper than their
roofs since the wading trunks and sealant prevented water from flooding
ank.

A M4 tank of Co. A, 746th Tank Bn. passes through St. Sauveur-le-
Vicomte during the fighting in Normandy in June 1944. This unit was used
to support the 82nd Airborne Division during the initial June fighting.

A M4 tank, probably from the 70th Tank Battalion, supporting troops during fighting in the Carentan area on 7 July 1944. This is a relatively early
duction M4 with the initial gun mantlet configuration without the side cheek armor. It has been rebuilt with the added hull and turret armor, probably in
land. The use of the prominent Allied star was common in the initial phases of the Normandy fighting, but they were later painted out by most units since
y provided too inviting a target to German gunners.

On 14 July 1944, a pair of armored recovery vehicles are used recover a burned M4 tank from C 3rd Armored Div. during the inte fighting around Le Desert earlier in week.

A pair of French children wave to the crew of a passing M4 tank moving through the town of St. Paul du Verney, east of the fighting for St. Lo on 17 July 1944. At this stage of the Normandy campaign, the M4 and M4A1 tanks with 75mm gun were the only types of medium tanks in service with the First Army.

A well camouflaged M4 of the Tank Battalion is passed by a me jeep during the preparations Operation "Cobra", the US break from the Normandy beach-he During the Normandy fighting, the Tank Battalion provided support to 4th Infantry Division.

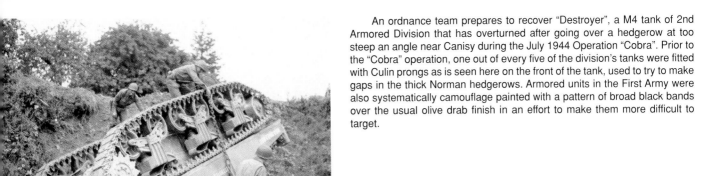

An ordnance team prepares to recover "Destroyer", a M4 tank of 2nd Armored Division that has overturned after going over a hedgerow at too steep an angle near Canisy during the July 1944 Operation "Cobra". Prior to the "Cobra" operation, one out of every five of the division's tanks were fitted with Culin prongs as is seen here on the front of the tank, used to try to make gaps in the thick Norman hedgerows. Armored units in the First Army were also systematically camouflage painted with a pattern of broad black bands over the usual olive drab finish in an effort to make them more difficult to target.

One of the key pieces of equipment during Operation ["C]ora" was the M1 bulldozer blade, seen here fitted to [Apa]che", from Co. A, 70th Tank Battalion near Tribehou on [21] July 1944. Although the Culin prongs are more famous [as a] means to break through the Norman hedgerows, the [bull]dozer blades were in fact more effective. Each of the [sep]arate tank battalions was provided with five or six tank [doz]ers for the "Cobra" breakout.

A M4 fitted with the Culin prongs passes by a M10 3-inch gun motor carriage during the opening phases of Operation "Cobra" in late July 1944. Although [the]re was much publicity about the Culin prongs, many veterans have said that the devices did not work very well in breaking through the thick Norman [he]dgerows.

One of the new M4A1 (76) is ·
breaking over the top of a hedge
near Pont Hebert during the ope
phases of Operation "Cobra". A tota
102 of these were split evenly betv
the 2nd and 3rd Armored Divis
when first delivered on 22 July 194
was hoped that the 76mm gun wou
the trick in dealing with the Ger
Panther tank, but Operation "Co
showed that it was inadequate w
dealing with the well angled fro
armor of the Panther.

A M4A1 (76) of the 33rd Arm'd Regt., 3rd Armored Div. in combat near Reffuveille on 7 August 1944. The success of Operation "Cobra" pushed the US Army out of the restrictive hedgerow country along the coast into the more open pastures of Brittany where the armored divisions could maneuver.

A M4A1 fitted with a M1 bulldozer blade is used to clean up debris
French town. The heavy air bombardment that preceded "Cobra" cau
havoc to French towns in its path, and the bulldozers were instrumenta
clearing roads for following waves of troops.

A M4A1 (76) of the 67th Arr
Regt., 2nd Armored Div. passes thro
Sever Calvados on 3 August 19
during the Normandy break-out. Cl
inspection of the turret roof shows
edge of the large Allied star painted
the roof to help in aerial identificati
Operation "Cobra" was the first ti
that US Army began to use fluoresc
red and yellow air identification par
for air recognition purposes.

A M4A1 dozer tank is used to clean up the ruins in Lonlay-L'Abbaye on ~~ugust~~ 1944 during the pursuit of the German army towards Paris. To the ~~behind~~ the tank, a T2 armored recovery vehicle can be seen.

While the US First and Third Armies were conducting the pursuit following the Normandy breakout, the US Seventh Army landed on the southern French coast near Marseilles as part of Operation "Dragoon" to unhinge the German defenses in central and western France. This is one of the M4A1 DD amphibious tanks of the 753rd Tank Battalion landed near St. Tropez. This shows the canvas floatation collar folded down after the tank has reached shore.

The collapse of German defenses ~~France~~ in mid-August led to a rapid ~~ed~~ drive to eastern France and the ~~gian~~ frontier. Here, infantry scurry ~~t~~ a well camouflaged M4 tank during ~~et~~ fighting by Patton's Third Army in ~~wn~~ along the Marne on 31 August ~~4~~.

By mid September, Patton's Third Army reached the Moselle river and began efforts to ma crossing in force. The northern crossing of the Mo took place near the town of Dieulouard. Here a bulldozer tank is used to create a roadway acro narrow tributary of the Moselle river on 12 Septem

As the lead element in Patton's northern thrust into Lorraine, the 7th Armored Division was the first to reach the fortress city of Metz. This is a forward observer tank of the 440th Armored Field Artillery Bn. which would travel with lead elements of the division and radio back information to the howitzer batteries for fire missions. (Patton Museum)

This M4 (76) of the 749th Tank Battalion was disabled near Char on 12 September during the fighting between the US 79th Division and German 16th Infantry Division. An anti-personnel mine has gone off u the second bogie assembly, severing the track.

Patton's forces surrounded provincial capital of Lorraine at Na and the 4th Armored Division got the Moselle river near Bayon. Her M4 medium tank of the 737th Battalion fires on buildings Dombasle, along the left flank of advance on 15 September 194 support of the 320th Infantry which crossing a nearby canal at the time

Although the [...]mans destroyed [...] of the bridges [...] the Moselle, the [...] Army's engineers [...]ly created pontoon [...]dway bridges [...]cient for tanks to [...]s. Here on 16 [...]ember, an M4 [...]ses the Moselle on [...]readway bridge, [...] in the [...]ground, the [...]royed local bridge [...]e seen.

A burned out M4A1 tank is recovered by a M25 Dragon Wagon on 22 September. This tank shows the wider mantlet adopted on the M34A1 gun mount on later production M4A1 tanks.

In response to Patton's attacks, Hitler ordered a panzer counter-attack [...]orraine by four of the new panzer brigades. These attacks culminated in [...]eries of intense tank battles around Arracourt on 21-27 September. Here, [...]4 has its transmission serviced in a forested work area during the [...]ting.

Another view of the Third Army's forested tank workshop, this time with the turret of a M4 removed for servicing the hull. The turret basket can be seen on the ground beyond the tank, while the turret itself is propped up on logs.

While Patton moved into Lorraine, Dever's Seventh Army to the south advanced towards Alsace and to the Swiss border. This is a pair of M4 tank Co. B, 756th Tank Battalion, veterans of the Italian campaign, knocked out during the fighting near Vesovi on 12 September 1944 as Third and Seventh A were attempting to link-up.

A crew of a M4A1 of the 75 Tank Battalion enjoys the jubilatio the French crowds as the Seve Army moved through St. Marie or September. This tank is a veteran o Italian campaign, and carries characteristic Mediterranean style the shipping code marking on its bc

September 1944
ne of the wettest
ecord in Europe,
many fields being
d to mud by the
Here, a M4 of the
Armored Field
ry Bn. HQ
any is retrieved
a wrecker after
g become bogged
in a field near
bieres on 26
ember 1944.

The crew of a M4 (105) assault gun of the HQ company, 191st Tank Bn.
food during a lull in the fighting near Rambervillers, France on 15
ber 1944. The M4(105) was fitted with a 105mm howitzer instead of the
al 75mm gun, and was used to provide indirect fire support for the
lion. In 1944, most tank battalions had six of these attached to the HQ
bany.

The 14th Armored Division was one of the last US armored divisions to
e in France, docking at Marseilles on 31 October 1944. It was
mitted to the fighting in the Vosges region of France on 20 November
4, and here, some M4A3 tanks of its Combat Command A move forward
r Cirey, France on 23 November 1944.

The M4 (105) assault gun was a prodigious consumer of ammunition
since it was normally used on fire support missions like normal field artillery.
Here, one of the crewman helps load a 105mm round through the shell
ejection port on the left turret side. The stenciled "5698GG" is a shipping
code for the unit.

The rainy conditions in the autumn of 1944 undermined roads, and led to accidents like this one where a M4A3 (76) of Co. A, 781st Tank Bn. slid off the road in Lamberg after the bank collapsed under its weight. It is being recovered by one of the new M32 armored recovery vehicles. Tank units in the Seventh Army sector in Alsace often used their shipping codes in place of normal bumper codes. In this case, the shipment code "9603-D" can be seen to the left of the Allied star.

The effect of a panzerfaust anti-tank rocket could be catastroph[.] detonated the internal ammunition of an M4. This M4A2 of the Frenc Armored Division serving with the US 6th Army Group in Alsace had its blown off after a panzerfaust set off its ammunition during the fighti Issans on 18 November 1944. The tank's hull can be seen in the dista[.]

During the 1944-45 fighting, some tank units were provided with the 60-tube, 4.5 inch T34 "Calliope" tank rocket launcher. This one is serving with 14th Armored Div. near Dettwiller on 16 February 1945. The T34 was not popular with tank units as it suffered from frequent misfires, and had exces[.] dispersion at range. Most tank units felt that its missions were better performed by normal artillery units.

While Patton's Third Army pushed
Lorraine, Hodge's First Army
ed into Belgium. A M4A1 (76) of
rd Armored Div. passes by the
ng wreck of a German truck in
ncheul-au-Bac near Cambrai on
ay to the Belgian frontier.

Here, an M4 from the 3rd Armored
Division burns in the outskirts of Mons,
Belgium while M5A1 light tanks push
ahead in a race for the German border.
In less than two weeks, the First Army
would reach the German frontier near
Aachen.

A M4 with M1 dozer clears debris
a road near Harze, Belgium. The
is covered with chalked greetings
Belgian citizens from one of the
nboring towns.

A M4A1 (76) of the 3rd Arm Div. gingerly moves down embankment on to a treadway b erected over pontoons on the M river near Liege, Belgium o September 1944 while local ci watch. The pontoon bridge was er alongside the ruins of a b demolished by the retreating Ger as can be seen by the abutment right.

During a lull in the fighting in Belgium on 30 September 1944, the crew of a M4A1 takes the opportunity to clean the gun barrel of their tank.

The northern flank of the First Army extended into the Netherlands. Here, a M4A1 (76) of Co. F, 66th Arm'd Regt., 2nd Armored Div. passes through a medieval arch in the town of Valkenberg on 17 September.

On 6 October 1944, the crew of a M4 tank of the 7th Armored Div. ordnance repair crews swap out a Continental R975 radial engine. radial aircraft engine powered both the M4 and M4A1 versions o Sherman tank.

In anticipation of encounters with bunkers the German Siegfried line, elements of First Army were provided with flame- ers. Four E4-5 flame-throwers were fitted A1 (76) tanks of 70th Tank Battalion on 11 ember 1944. These tanks had previously t in the Belgian campaign, and the ed inscriptions of Belgian civilians can be on the hull side during this training cise on 13 September. Two of these tanks temporarily attached to the 741st Tank lion and were used to attack a German x three days later. This configuration was d seriously inadequate as the tank had to ach to within 25 yards of the pillbox, and after using up its fuel, the pillbox was not ked out.

On 13 September 1944, Task Force X of the 3rd Armored Division penetrated the Siegfried line near Roeten Germany, south of Aachen led by a Scorpion flail tank. The unit had found one of the gaps in the defense line designed to permit German troops to pass through that had not been properly sealed up after the retreat. This is a view two days later as one of the unit's M4 dozer tanks moves through the gap in the dragon's teeth.

Another view of a 3rd Armored Div. M4 ving troops of the 36th Armored Infantry iment while moving through border nses near Roeten on 15 September 1944.

Another view of the same M4 tank of the 735th Tank Battalion inside town of Roth with GIs from the 8th Infantry Regiment using the local te to provide cover from snipers.

On 15 September after penetrating through the Siegfried line, the 8th Infantry Regiment began a motorized advance on the Schnee Eifel ridgeline. Supported by M4 tanks of the 735th Tank Battalion, the spearhead came under fire near the town of Roth.

A composite hull M4 named "Dodo" of Co. D, 66th Arm'd Regt., 2nd Armored Div. crosses a treadway bridge over a stream during operations along the German frontier.

The town of Schevenhuette was the s intense fighting when the German Sev Army launched a local counter-attack o September 1944. Tanks of the 3rd Arm Division move through the town on September after the fighting ended in bl stalemate.

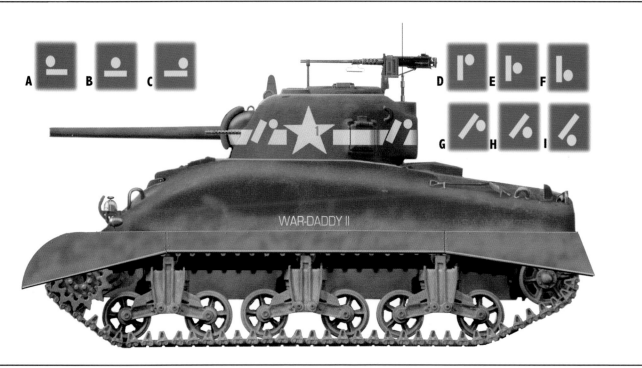

A1, Co. G, 3rd Battalion, 1st Armored Regt., 1st Armored Division, Kasserine Pass, Tunisia, February 1943

This M4A1 shows the markings typical of US tanks in the early fighting in Tunisia. The markings are in yellow which was common Armored
e practice at the time. The division had an elaborate system of company and battalion markings using small geometric symbols. Insignia
ploying a bar and circle were from 1st Armored Regt. as seen here, those with a bar and square were from the 13th Armored Regt. As shown
e inset illustrations of the 1st Armored Regiment insignia, the three line companies in each battalion shared a common style of bar design,
the company signified by the location of the small circle. So 1st Bn. (Cos. A, B, C) used a horizontal bar, 2nd Bn. (Co. D, E, F) used a vertical
and 3rd Bn. (Cos. G, H, I) used an angled bar. Later in the Tunisian fighting, the divisions usually camouflaged the tanks with an improvised
t made from the local mud. This particular tank, "War Daddy II" was captured by the Germans after an ill-fated encounter with Tiger I tanks
Pz.Abt. 501 near Sbeitla. The vehicle registration number is in blue drab.

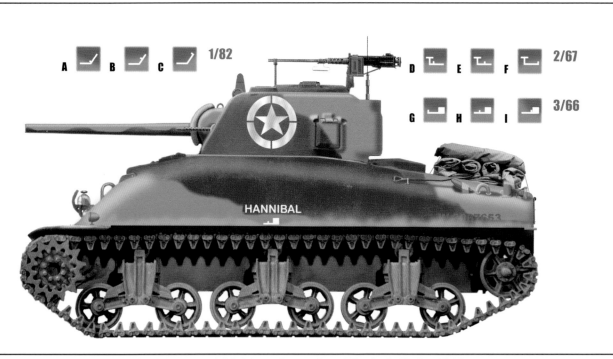

A1, Co. H, 66th Armored Regt., 2nd Armored Division, Operation "Husky", Sicily, 1943

Prior to the Sicily invasion, Operational Memo 34 was issued which instructed armored units to camouflage their tanks and other vehicles
a pattern of earth yellow or earth red over the usual olive drab. The 2nd Armored Division generally used earth yellow as seen here. This
sion had a complicated set of insignia to distinguish their sub-units, first applied during training at Ft. Benning in the US. This was usually carried
he side, and in the center of the bow. Each battalion had a basic insignia, and a small dash was added to the bottom line to distinguish the
e line companies in each. The inset drawings show samples from three typical units, the 1st Battalion, 82nd Recon, 2nd Battalion, 67th
nored, and 3rd Battalion, 66th Armored Regiment. Sicily saw the introduction of the "Allied Star", developed after it was found that the US star
gnia could be mistaken for a German cross at a distance. This was carried in 20-inch size on the turret side, turret roof, and front transmission
using, and a larger 60-inch star was carried on the engine deck. Another form of identification introduced for Operation "Husky" was the use
a pair of olive drab pennants, carried on the radio aerial. These are illustrated on the following Salerno print.

M4A1, Co. A, 191st Tank Battalion, Salerno landings, 9 September 1943

In 1943, the Allied Forces HQ ordered tank units participating in amphibious landings in Italy to add an enlarged white or yellow c around the white star, and some units took this to an extreme with very thick circles painted in yellow. Some of the tanks of this battalion had a tactical number painted in yellow on the turret front. The battalion followed the usual practices of naming the tanks starting with company letter, such as "Aces Up", "Adams", etc. The bumper codes on this vehicle were "5A 181^ A-9". Another form of identification wa use of a pair of olive drab pennants, flown from the top of radio mast. This practice had been started for the landings in Sicily, since it was fc that national markings often weren't visible after they became obscured by dust. The same pattern was used in the Salerno landings, with pennants being flown.

M4A1, Co. F, 13th Armored Regt., 1st Armored Division, Anzio beach-head, Italy, March 1944

By the time of the Anzio landings, the 1st Armored Division had reverted to a simpler system of markings. Each company in a battalion u a color in succession, red, white, and blue. Each platoon carried the appropriate number of vertical stripes, with the headquarters comp using a horizontal stripe. So in the case of the 2nd Battalion/13th Armored Regt., D company used red, E company used white and F comp (as seen here) used blue. The tank name started in the company letter. This division followed the camouflage patterns suggested in FM-5-: adding a pattern of earth red over olive drab, with white counter-shading under the gun barrel, and sometimes under the sponsons. By this ti the 1st Armored Division left the star off prominent positions since they made too clear an aiming point. The circled stars were carried on turret roof.

A1, Co. B, 760th Tank Battalion, US Fifth Army, Italy, January 1944

This is "Big John", the M4A1 of the commander of Co. B, 740th Tank Battalion. Capt. John Krebs was decorated with the Silver Star for his
...ership during the attack on Mt. Porchia on 6 January 1944. Like most of the tanks in the battalion, the markings are fairly simple. The stars
...e all been painted out. The tanks in B company all used names starting in "B" such as: "Big Bertha", "Bama", "Babe", "Bayu", "Bono", "Berlin
... Back", "Berlin or Bust", etc. Most of the tanks still carried the shipping designator marking from embarkation in Italy, which was a pattern of
...e colored bars and a letter. As shown in the inset drawing, this was carried on the right rear engine access door. It was also carried in the
... on the center of the transmission housing. Other markings on the rear door is the old pattern subdued bridging weight symbol, a "20" in a
...circle, and a caution marking in white. The tank also carries the usual bumper codes on the front of the hull and the lower lip of the rear hull
...erstructure, "5A 760^ B-13".

, Co. C, 756th Tank Battalion, Monte Cassino, Italy, February 1944

Many tanks in Italy were camouflage painted, often a pattern of earth yellow or earth red over olive drab. After combat experience, many
...k battalions painted out or otherwise obscured the large Allied star insignia as it provided too prominent an aiming point and made the tank
...easily visible. In this case, the crew appears to have tried to suppress the marking using dirt or engine grease. This battalion used a simple
...of tactical marking consisting of a set of bars to indicate the platoon. The tactical numbers were often repeated on the rear of the turret,
...arated by a small circled Allied star in the fashion of "1*3", etc. The bumper codes on this vehicle were "5A 756^ C-14".

M4, Co. C, 70th Tank Battalion, Utah Beach, Normandy, France, D-Day, 6 June 1944

This M4 took part in the Normandy landings and became bogged down in a sink hole. It is fitted with deep wading trunks which w
removed later in the day after the tank was extracted from the hole and put back into action. To make the tank waterproof, canvas sealed
mastic glue was liberally applied over opening including the turret ring and hatches, as can be seen from the dark band around the turret
side shell ejection port. This company later supported the 101st Airborne Div. in the fighting around St. Mere Eglise. While preparing for the inva
in England, the battalion adopted the mascot of "Joe Peckerwood", a cartoon figure of a turtle in a tanker's helmet with a ribbon read
"Soixante-Dix" (Seventy in French) across his chest. This was painted on all the battalion's armored vehicles prior to the landings as a wo
distinguish the unit. The 70th Tank Bn. also made use of the practice of painting a large red tactical number on the hull or turret side.

M4, 37th Tank Battalion, 4th Armored Division, Brittany, France, July 1944

This was the M4 commanded by Captain Bill Dwight, the assistant S3 and battalion liaison officer. Like nearly all of the tanks in the battal
it had a cartoon painted on the hull side, in this case, the Lone Ranger's side-kick, Tonto from the popular radio show. As in the case of many
the cartoon's, the cartoon was superimposed on the tri-color triangle of the US Armored Force. This tank was knocked out during the fight
near Commercy, but put back into action with Co. B.

A1 (76), Co. F, 33rd Armored Regt., 3rd Armored Division, Belgium, September 1944

The 3rd Armored Division, like the 2nd Armored Division, generally carried tactical numbers on the turret in chrome yellow. In addition, a tank
e, beginning with the company letter was standard, in this case, "Ferocious III". On 2 September 1944, CCA of 3rd Armored Division liberated
Belgian town of Mesvin near Mons. The following day, some of the tanks were decorated by the town's people with greetings in white chalk
en here.

A3 (76), Co. C, 761st Tank Battalion (Colored), Task Force Rhine, Germany 1945

This is a tank of the famous "Black Panthers", the best known of the segregated tank battalions. This unit served in the north-west Europe
paign and received the Presidential Unit Citation. This particular tank was commanded by Sgt. Daniel Cardell, and named "Cool Stud Inc."
name came from the company mascot, a rooster, that was carried by the crew. This was Cardell's fourth tank, the other three having been
n action. The turret carries the name of Cardell's wife. There are two lines above it which appear to be crew member names, the gunner
Luther Goffe, and Pvt. Leonard Smith, loader. The driver and co-driver T5 Horace Clark and T4 Linson Ball, were painted in small letters on the
is plate in front of their hatches. At the time, this tank was fitted with metal grouser tracks with duck-bill extenders.

M4A3 (76), 19th Tank Battalion, 9th Armored Division, Belgium, November 1944

Starting in November 1944, the 602nd Camouflage Engineer Battalion began a systematic process of camouflaging tanks in the 12th A
Group. First, the tanks were camouflage painted. This usually consisted of black over the usual olive drab, but on some occasions w
additional paint was available, a third color was used as is seen with the light green pattern here. After this was done, a set of steel rods w
welded to the hull front and side, and the turret sides, to which was attached Sommerfield matting, a type of screening. The screen was inten
to make it easier for the crew to attach tree branches for camouflage. By this stage of the war, many battalions completely painted over
national insignia.

M4A3E2, Co. C, 37th Tank Battalion, 4th Armored Division, Bastogne, Belgium, December 1944

This is the Jumbo assault tank commanded by Lt. Charles P. Boggess which led the spearhead of Patton's Third Army in the counter-att
to relieve Bastogne during the Battle of the Bulge. The slogan "First in Bastogne" was chalked on the sides after the task force reached Basto
on 26 December 1944. The markings are otherwise simple, including the tank name "Cobra King", the vehicle registration number, and var
shipping stencils. The 37th Tank Battalion continued to use the white star long after most other battalions had painted it over. This tank was fit
with rubber chevron tracks and duck-bill extenders.

A1, 709th Tank Battalion, 75th Infantry Division, Colmar, France, February 1945

This old M4A1 was one of the tanks taking part in the counter-attack against the German Operation "Nordwind" offensive in Alsace in uary 1945. Most of the US and French tanks during this campaign were painted with white-wash winter camouflage, often quite hastily lied as is the case here. The old vehicle registration number in blue drab is barely visible on the rear side.

A3E2, 756th Tank Battalion, 31st Infantry Division, Ostheim, Alsace, France, January 1945

This Jumbo took part in the counterattacks by the US Seventh Army against German forces in Alsace following the failed German Operation "Nordwind" nsive. The markings are simple, and consist of the tactical number "X3" on the hull side, and a small name painted lower on the side. This shows the use e standardized system for welding Sommerfield matting to the hull and turret for the attachment of foliage, in this case, pine boughs.

M4A3 (76), 760th Tank Battalion, US Fifth Army, Italy 1945

This is "Kokomo" the M4A3(76) command tank of the 760th Tank Battalion during the fighting in northern Italy in January 1945. The battalion began receiving M4A3 tanks with the 76mm gun in the autumn of 1944. Since US infantry was more familiar with the short-barreled 75mm tanks, the battalion usually marked the new tanks prominently with white stars to avoid confusion with long-barreled German tanks. In 1945, it was operated by Major C. S. "Trim" Curtis when he took over command of the battalion in December 1944. Command tanks and other special vehicles in the battalion did not follow the practice of using the first letter of the company in the name.

M4A3E8, CCA, 4th Armored Division, Germany, February 1945

This is the command tank of Col. Creighton Abrams, who by this time had been transferred from command of the 37th Tank Battalion to head the division's Combat Command A. Abrams was one of the most successful US tank commanders of World War II, and the current M1 tank is named in his honor. His tanks since training in Britain had been named "Thunderbolt", and this was his seventh tank, the others having been lost in combat or having been worn out. The tank has been fitted with applique armor on the glacis plate, turret front, and hull sides, as became a standard practice in Patton's Third Army after the Battle of the Bulge.

A M4 tank of the 3/67th Arm'd Regt., 2nd Armored Div. stands guard in an entrenchment on 10 October 1944. Having fought through the Siegfried line, [f]ront turned into a stalemate by early October. This M4 is of the later production type with the M34A1 gun mount, and a full set of hull and turret applique [armo]r. The attachment of a spare 10 gallon oil can on the right fender was common practice in some tank units in 1944. By October, the practice of applying [swirl]s of black over the tank's olive drab finish had become standard practice in the First Army and can be seen here.

Due to shortages of US minefield breaching equipment, the US Army obtained small numbers of Crab flails from the British. They were first used by a [plat]oon of the 747th Tank Battalion during Operation "Cobra" in July 1944. Due to the small number available, the US Army frequently requested the [assi]stance of the British 79th Armoured Div. to provide flail tank support, and this Crab is in use near Breinig, Germany on 11 October 1944.

The short-range street fighting along the German border in October 1944 saw far more extensive use of German panzerfaust anti-tank rockets. [A] result, US tank units began adding sand-bags to the glacis plate of the tank in an attempt to improve protection. This is a M4 of the 3rd Armored Div. car[rying] troops of the 36th Infantry during operations near Stolberg on 14 October 1944.

A T2 armored recovery vehicle provides assistance in repairing [a] tank of the 66th Arm'd Regt., 2nd Armored Div. in the city of Als[dorf,] Germany on 15 October 1944. The crew appears to be replacing the [smooth] rubber block tracks seen on the left side with T49 metal grouser track. O[nce] the wet autumn weather arrived in 1944, the smooth rubber block [track] developed a reputation as "suicide track" since it provided poor tracti[on in] the mud.

The crew of "Idle" from 3/66th Arm'd Regt., 2nd Armored Div. do their daily chores in the outskirts of Alsdorf, Germany on 15 October 1944. While some of the crew do suspension repair, one of the crewman shaves.

The first major German city to come under attack on the western front was Aachen, starting on 11 October 1944. A counterattack by the 3rd Panzer Gren. Div. on 15 October is met here by elements of the 26th Infantry Regt., 1st Infantry Div., supported by M4 tanks of the 745th Tank Battalion. The M4 on the left is still fitted with its wading trunk from the landing in Normandy.

The fighting in Aachen was intense and costly. Here an M4 provides watch as a M10 tank destroyer moves forward on 20 October. The [Ger]man troops finally surrendered the next day when a M12 155mm gun [moto]r carriage was used to reduce the commander's bunker at point blank [rang]e.

The intense fighting along the Siegfried line and in Aachen convinced the US Army of the need for a more heavily armored tank to provide close support. A solution was already in the works since February 1944 in the form of the M4A3E2 "Jumbo". This tank had the same 75mm gun as the normal M4, but had thicker armor on the turret and hull. This is a Jumbo in one of the ordnance yards in France on 4 November 1944 being prepared after shipment for issuance to a tank unit. It provides a good view of the new turret and the thick gun mantlet.

A good example of the Jumbo in [serv]ice. This is a M4A3E2 of the 743rd [Tan]k Bn., supporting the 30th Infantry [Divi]sion near Altdorf, Germany on 27 [Nov]ember 1944. It has been reinforced [with] additional sand-bag armor on the [glac]is plate, which was then covered [with] camouflage netting.

One of the main problems fa
tank crew in the autumn of 1944
the poor mobility of the M4 in m
conditions. This new M4A3 (76)
completely bogged down in the
while supporting the 84th Div
during fighting in Germany or
November 1944.

This rear view of the same M4A3 (76) tank shows that it is fitted with the T49 metal grouser tracks, one of the better solutions for muddy conditions compared to the rubber block track but still far from perfect.

The M4's floatation problem in mud became even worse after troops began adding improvised sand-bag armor on the hull front and sides. This is a M4A3 (76) of the 743rd Tank Bn. near Eschweiler, Germ in November 1944.

The solution to the floata
problem was to attach extenders to
track end connectors, and these car
seen on this tank from C/69th Tank
6th Armored Div. These were gi
various nicknames by the troops s
as "duck bills" or "duck feet".

Troops from the 531st Heavy Maintenance (Tanks) Co. tighten the track on on a M4A3 (105) at the maintenance yard in Etain France on 27 ...mber 1944. They have just added duck-bill extenders to the track.

The crew of a new M4A3 (105) assault gun shown above try out the new duck bill extenders in the yard at the Etain tank depot in November 1944.

Another problem that was ...ressed in the autumn of ...4 was the poor camouflage ...cipline of US tank crews. ...e First Army decided that ... best solution would be for ...cialized engineer troops to ...e care of the matter. As a ...ult, starting in October, the ...nd Engineer Camouflage ...talion developed a ...ndardized method for ...lying camouflage paint to ... tanks, and adding a layer ...Sommerfield matting over ... main surfaces for the ...achment of foliage. Entire ...k battalions were painted ...ing refits. The usual ...nouflage was black over ...e drab, but some units had ...er colors added if paint was ...ailable.

This photo shows the 602nd Engineer Camouflage Battalion welding Sommerfield matting to the side of a M4A3 (76). Surprisingly, this tank still has sand shields fitted. There was an official policy in 12th Army Group to have sand-shields removed as they interfered with maintenance.

This is a good example of a M4 named "Bucks" near Eupen, Germ on 8 November 1944 after the Sommerfield matting has been added.

One of the most serious tactical shortcomings in US tanks was the difficulty in communicating with neighboring infantry. The tank radios could not communicate with the infantry's radios. The solution was either to rack mount an infantry radio like the SCR-300 into some tanks, or to attach an exterior phone to the tank. This is a M4 of the 709th Tank Bn. with an exterior phone added inside a .30 cal metal ammunition box. It is put to use during operations with the 81st Division near Zweifall on 24 November 1944.

The US Army still segregated World War II and extended to tank u as well. Two black battalions saw com service in northw Europe in 1944. 761st Tank Bn. is more famous, receiv the Presidential Citation for its con performance. This M4A3 (76) of the operating near Na France on 5 Novem 1944.

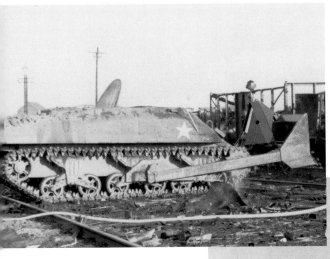

Some derelict tanks were later converted to other chores. This M4A1 hull has been fitted with a M1 dozer for use by Transportation Corps units in the railroad marshalling yard at Ramilles, Belgium in late 1944.

The rainy conditions in the autumn of 1944 are graphically shown in this view of a M4 (105) assault gun of the 756th Tank Battalion seen near Les Rouges Eaux on 8 November 1944.

Surrendering German troops pass near a M4 tank of Co. C, 735th Tank Battalion near Vigny, France during the fighting in the Saar region on 10 November 1944.

Tank units frequently used the shelter of small towns when not committed to the fighting. These are M4A3 tanks of the 10th Armored Division on the streets of Tetange, Luxembourg on 13 November 1944.

A M4A1 of the 2nd Armored Division passes through Beggendorf o November 1944, one of the towns taken in the Aachen fighting that se as First Army's salient towards the Roer river. The tank is carrying which were used to drop under the tanks as unditching beams if the tan stuck in the mud. This was a common practice in the division during November 1944 Roer river offensive.

During the Roer river offensive in late November 1944, the 84th Division was the northernmost US unit in Europe, rubbing shoulders with the Br 43rd Infantry Division to its north. The town of Geilenkirchen straddled the British and US zones, so the British provided tank support for US infa operations in the town as seen here on 19 November 1944 with British Shermans providing fire support for the GIs.

Laying next to the Dutch border, Geilenkirchen was the start of a major ☐ of German fortifications and mine fields. So British Crab flail tanks ☐ed the 84th Division clear approaches near the town during the 19 ☐ember 1944 fighting.

While not as common a practice as in Italy, tanks in northwest Europe were sometimes used to provide indirect artillery fire support. This M4A1 of the 32nd Arm'd Regt., 3rd Armored Div. along with other tanks from the unit are being used as improvised artillery during the Roer river offensive on 19 November 1944.

A M4A1 dozer tank from Co. I, 66th Arm'd Regt., 2nd Armored Div. ☐rs a road during Roer river offensive on 19 November 1944. The M1 ☐er assembly has been damaged during use, and the frame attaching the ☐le has been badly bent.

The turret interior of the M4 was more spacious on the left side to ☐mit the loader to access the gun. This is a view down into the loader's ☐ion of an M4 of the 774th Tank Bn. near Welfrang, Luxembourg on 20 ☐vember 1944. He is placing rounds in the forward ready rack. The co-☐al .30 cal machine gun breech can be seen immediately above his left ☐ulder, and the gun breech to the right of the photo.

An evocative picture of the harsh field conditions during the winter 1944 fighting in Germany as two GIs huddle under the shelter of a M4 tank. This tank has been fitted with an external tank telephone as can be seen in the form of the .30 cal. ammo box attached to the engine door above the head of the GI to the right.

A M4 (105) assault gun of the 3rd Armored Division sits well concealed under improvised camouflage in the ruins of Eschweiler, Germany on 26 November 1944 during the Roer river offensive.

As in the case of the 2nd Armored Div., the 771st Tank Bn. had suff from enough experiences of bogged down tanks that its tanks ca unditching logs during the Roer fighting. These are the M4 (105) ass guns of the HQ company in Welz, Germany on 29 November 1944. Altho there were plans to equip all tanks in the operation with duck bills, there neither enough time or equipment to do so.

The ground is littered with spent 105mm howi casings near a M4 (105) assault gun of the company, 70th Tank Bn. providing fire support du the fighting near Schevenhutte, Germany or December 1944.

The crew of a M4 tank of the 2nd Armored Divis attach duck bills to their tank track during a refi Baesweiller, Germany on 5 December 1944. The e connectors without duck bills can be seen in the foreground, the end connectors with duck bills are se on the track to the right.

In the autumn of 1944, two tank [bat]talions, the 738th and 739th, were [conve]rted into specialized tank battalions [for th]e use of minefield clearing equipment. [Each] had a company with 18 T1E1 mine [roller]s, two companies with 12 T1E3 mine [roller] tanks, and six dozer tanks. The 739th [Tank] Bn. (Special) was deployed with the [Ninth] Army on 24 November 1944. This M4 [is fitt]ed with the T1E3 mine rollers and is [passi]ng through Beggendorf, Germany on [12 De]cember 1944.

There was some concern that the added weight of the mine rollers would wreck treadway bridges. So the 739th Tank Bn. (Special) sent a T1E3 roller tank to a local engineer battalion to test the effect of the added weight.

[This] front view of a T1E3 mine roller tank [passi]ng across a treadway bridge provides an [inter]esting look at the mounting assembly in the [cent]er of the rig.

Shortages of equipment occasionally le[d] substitution. This M4A3 (76) is being used by the [?] Tank Destroyer Battalion in Gurzenich, Germany d[uring] the fighting there on 14 December 1944. The bat[talion] was normally equipped with the M10 3-in gun [motor] carriage.

A GI peers inside a M4 which has slid into a water-filled hole in the ruins of Duren, Germany during the fighting there in December 1944.

A T2 arm[ored] recovery vehicle o[f the] 463rd Ordnance [Co.] tows a M4 tank o[f the] 746th Tank Bn. tha[t] struck a mine. [The] mine has comple[tely] blown off the lead b[ogie] assembly. The [T2] appears to [be] impressively arm[ed] but in fact the 7[5mm] hull gun and 3[7mm] turret gun are dum[mies] intended to mak[e it] appear like the no[rmal] M3 medium tank [on] which it was based[.]

52

The HQ company of 2/32nd Arm'd Regt., 3rd Armored Div. move forward near Marche, Belgium on 31 December 1944. The tanks are M4 (105) assault
, while to the right is a M3A1 half-track.

(105) assault guns of the HQ company of 2/32nd Arm'd Regt. provide fire support during operations on 3 January 1945 in Belgium.

Tanks of the 2nd Armored Div. support the 84th Division during the fighting near Amonines, Belgium on 2 January 1945. The lead tank appears to composite hull M4. It is fitted with the T54 metal chevron tracks with duck bill extenders. There was quite a bit of variation in the detail of the duck bill many were manufactured locally in shops in Belgium and France.

The crew of "Come In", a M4 (76) of C/22nd Tank Bn., 11th Arm Div., do maintenance on their tank while bivouacked near Joden Belgium on 5 January 1945.

A M4 (76mm) of the 750th Tank Bn. provides support for the 290th Infantry Regt., 75th Division in positions near Beffs, Belgium on 7 January 1945.

This M4 of the 747th Tank Battalion knocked out six German tanks before itself being knocked out during combat in support of the 29th Division in early January 1945. The tank is pock-marked with small caliber hits, probably from a 20mm anti-aircraft cannon.

"Kathleen" a M4 (76) of Co. B, 41st Tank Battalion receives a coat of e wash camouflage on 10 January 1945 while bivouacked in Bereneux, ium.

A M4A3 (76) leads a column from the 712th Tank Bn. during operations near Bavigne, Luxembourg on 12 January 1945. It is fitted with T48 rubber vron track with duck bill extenders.

The crews of a p[ ] M4 (76) of the 771st [ ] Bn. peer off into [ ] distance at a Ger[ ] artillery strike on [ ] outskirts of Berism[ ] Belgium, on 14 Jan[ ] 1945 while supporting [ ] 84th Division in the [ ] Like most separate [ ] battalions at this stag[ ] the war, the vehicles [ ] very plainly marked an[ ] stars have been pa[ ] over.

GIs of Co. C, 23rd Armored Infantry Bn., 7th Armored Div. wait for orders in the streets of St. Vith, center of some of the most intense fighting of the Battle of the Bulge. The M4A3 in the background has been camouflaged painted with temporary whitewash.

The crew of a M4A1 (76) of the [ ] Armored Div. add foliage to their tan[ ] an effort to improve its camouflage [ ] Kiewelbach, Luxembourg on [ ] January 1945. This tank is fitted [ ] metal chevron track and duck bill [ ] extenders.

It was rare to see US and British tanks together on the same mission. The exception was along the border of the US 9th Army and the British 21st Army [Grou]p where the two allies met. Here, an American M4 can be seen near a British Churchill during a joint attack against the town of Brachelen on 26 January [1945]

In the wake of the Ardennes offensive, the Germans launched Operation "Nordwind" against US and French forces in Alsace. This is a snow camouflaged M4A3 (76) of the 709th Tank Bn. supporting the 75th Division during the fighting in Alsace in February 1945.

US tankers were not pleased by the poor armor protection [of th]e M4. After the Battle of the Bulge, Patton's Third Army [deci]ded to initiate a program of uparmoring M4s with armor [plat]e taken from knocked out American and German tanks as an [alte]rnative to the ineffective use of sand bags. The [impr]ovements were carried out by ordnance companies starting [in F]ebruary 1945. This is a good example of a M4A3 (76) [stati]oned with the 303rd MP Co. at Patton's HQ in Luxembourg [City.] The glacis plate came straight off another M4, complete [with] the various attachments and fittings.

The failure of the German Arde
offensive crippled the German army
ensured Germany's defeat. Although Ge
resistance was often fierce, there would b
serious check on US operations after Jar
1945. Here, infantry clamber onboard a N
(76) of the 2nd Armored Div. during Oper
"Grenade" near Aachen on 20 February 19

A scene all too common in the final months of the war in Germany, a knocked out M4A3 (76) of the 7th Armored Div. Many tanks were lost in skirmishes with small groups of German defenders armed with panzerfaust anti-tank rockets. About 11% of US tank casualties during the 1945 fighting were due to panzerfausts and other close range anti-tank weapons.

In February 1945, the ordna
workshops of Patton's Third Army began
armoring M4 tanks with armor from knocked
tanks. This is a M4A3E8 of the 4th Armd
Division with a typical package of armor on
hull and turret.

This is the M4A3E8 command tank of Col. Creighton Abrams of the 4th ....red Div. in March 1945. Like many tanks of Patton's Third Army, it has ... retrofitted with added armor on the hull front, hull sides, and turret. This ... seventh M4, named "Thunderbolt VII" as can be seen on the side ...que armor. (Patton Museum)

This other view of Abrams M4A3E8 gives a better view of the turret armor. Abrams crew also mounted a .30 cal machine gun on the cover over the gunner's sight. (Patton Museum)

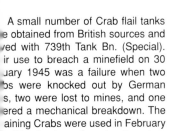

A small number of Crab flail tanks ... obtained from British sources and ...ved with 739th Tank Bn. (Special). ...ir use to breach a minefield on 30 ...uary 1945 was a failure when two ...bs were knocked out by German ...s, two were lost to mines, and one ...ered a mechanical breakdown. The ...aining Crabs were used in February ... March in attempts to clear ...efields on the approaches to the ...r and Rhine rivers. This is a Crab in ...ration near Vicht on the Roer river ...roaches on 21 February 1945.

The first M4A3E8 tanks b
being issued in January 1
These used the new H
suspension which improved
mobility of the M4 in muddy te
due to the use of a wider t
These two tankers from 66th A
Regt., 2nd Armored Div. are ta
part in a press briefing at Teu
Netherlands on 22 February
where they are showing
difference in size between
75mm and 76mm projectiles
standing in front of one of the
M4A3E8 tanks.

New or not, the M4A3E8 tanks were soon covered with applique armor in the form of sand-bags and spare track blocks. This is a tank of A/18th T
Bn., 8th Armored Div. at Bocholtz, Netherlands on 23 February 1945.

A M4 dozer tank of the 5th Armored Div. moves forward
~~gh~~ Ubach during the Operation "Grenade" on 24 February
.

A M4A3 (76) knocked out during the fighting in Germany late February 1945. The design of the Allied star is somewhat unusual. The tank is fitted with metal chevron tracks and duck bill extenders, as well as a full array of sand-bag armor on the glacis plate.

~~M~~4 (76) of Co. C, 771st Tank Bn. sets out from Linnich, Germany while supporting the 84th Division during the Roer offensive.

A M4 dozer tank cross[...] pontoon bridge over the [...] river on 24 February [...] Operation "Grenade" f[...] succeeded in overwhelmin[...] German defense along [...] Roer river after month[...] bloody fighting by the [...] Army.

A M4A1 (76) moves past one of the double Bailey bridges erected over the Roer near Julich. The tank is fitted with sand-bags on the glacis and carries several unditching beams on the nose.

A M4 named "Lil-Patty-Lou" of 2nd Armored Div. is directed by an [...] to the treadway bridge over the Roer [...] Julich on 26 February 1945.

A M4A3 (76) of the 701st Tank Bn. near [...]nich on 25 February. The unit had lost 22 [...] the day before to German anti-tank guns [...] obstacles while supporting the 405th [...]try near Hottorf, a bloody reminder that the [...]was not yet over.

A M4A3 of the 5th Armored Div. moves through Lovenich on 27 February 1945 during the exploitation phase of Operation "Grenade". The crew has created a large rack on the back of the turret to stow personal gear.

Tanks of the 5th Armored Div. form up in the outskirts of Rheindahlen, Germany on 1 March 1945. The jeep in the foreground has had improvised mud [...]ards added on either side.

Co. H, 67th Arm'd Regt., 2nd Armored Division pass through Priesterath, Germany on 28 February while on the way to the Rhine. This M4 is heavily decked in artillery camouflage net over the sand-bag applique armor. With ground conditions drying, the tanks are returning to the use of the T51 rubber block track, but fitted with duck bill extenders.

A rear view of the same column from 2nd Armored Div. in Prieste showing the typical heavy stowage on the rear deck.

A column of well camouflaged M4A3 tanks of 2nd Armored Div. move through Krefeld on 2 March 1945 during the assault towards the Rhine. Curiously enough, the second tank in the column is still fitted with a Culin hedgerow cutter.

A pair of tanks from the 2 Armored Division in Krefeld on 3 Mar during the advance on the Rhine. large amount of armor was se through the town as the positions on opposite side of the Rhine were held the Panzer Lehr Division.

A curious photo of a dozer tank of 66th Arm'd Regt., 2nd Armored Div. two large holes blown in the blade. Many units used dozer tanks to lead [colu]mns if M4A3E2 Jumbo assault tanks were not available, since the dozer [provid]ed a measure of stand-off protection against panzerfaust anti-tank [rock]ets.

Task Force Van Houton from CCB, 2nd Armored Division was given a rough reception during the fighting for Rheinberg on the west bank of the Rhine on 9 March 1945. German anti-tank guns and panzerfausts knocked out 39 of the 54 tanks used in the attack. This M4A3 took five hits, one of them completely shearing off the left drive sprocket.

Crews from the 2nd Armored Div. try to [pry] open the hatch of a M4A3 knocked out [in th]e street fighting in Rheinberg to free a [wou]nded crewman. The attack was so [cost]ly due to the lack of supporting infantry [and] the expectation that the town would not [be] so heavily defended.

One of the new M4A3E8 tanks oper
with the 8th Armored Div. near Roermund
February 1945. Some of the tanks were
fitted with the muzzle brake so often assoc
with this type.

A column of M4A3 tanks of the 748th Tank
Bn. pass by a knocked out StuG III assault gun
in Replen, Germany on 6 March 1945 while
supporting the 35th Division.

The HQ company of the 736th Tank
prepares 105mm ammunition for their M4 (1
assault guns while supporting the 83rd Divis
near Neuss, Germany on 3 March 1945.
ammunition came packed in the fiberbo
tubular containers seen on the ground.

In preparation for expected river [cros]sing operations over the Rhine, a [numb]er of tank battalions were [provi]ded with DD tanks. This is a DD [tank] of the 781st Tank Bn. during a [pract]ice exercise near Binau with the [flot]ation collar being erected.

A DD tank from the 781st Tank Bn. enters the water after the floatation collar has been fully erected. The propellers can be seen at the rear of the tank. The 736th Tank Bn. swam 17 DD tanks across the Rhine on 24 March. But the 748th Tank Bn. with 51 DD tanks was only able to swim 8 over the Rhine due to damage to the floatation collars during transit.

A M4A3E2 of the 4th Armored [Divi]sion passes by a destroyed [Ger]man flak truck during the [figh]ting on the western side of the [Rhi]ne in March 1944. Although the [M4]A3E2 was issued with a 75mm [gun], Patton's Third Army units [rep]laced it with a 76mm gun [beg]inning in February 1945.

On 7 March, a task force of T26E3 heavy tanks from the 9th Armored Division was surprised to discover that the Ludendorff bridge at Remagen not been demolished like all of the other Rhine bridges. The German garrison finally detonated the demolition charges, but some failed to explode, and low grade commercial explosive that did detonate failed to drop the bridge. Here, a M4A3 tank of 14th Tank Bn. passes beyond the two eastern towers had housed machine gun positions for the defense of the bridge shortly after the capture of the east bank.

The crew of M4A3 (76) tank e lunch on the streets Leutesdorf as division expanded bridgehead over eastern bank of Rhine river on March 1945. The hu fitted with Sommerf matting.

A M4A3E2 Jumbo assault tank of the 37th Tank Bn., 4th Armored Div.
es thorough Alzey, Germany on 20 March 1945. This is another
nple of a M4A3E2 rearmed with a 76mm gun.

A camouflaged M4A3 moves up towards Limburg as the 9th Armored Division expands its Rhine bridgehead beyond Remagen on 27 March 1945.

M4A3 tanks of the 11th Armored Division wait near Andernach on the west side of the Rhine as the Remagen bridgehead is expanded. They are painted large tactical numbers on the hull side, peculiar to this unit.

The 8th Armored Division uses a mine in Lindford, Germany to act as a r facility for their vehicles. To the left, a M4A3E8 tank has its tracks repaired.

A M4 tank of Co. C, 735th Tank Bn. prepares to cross the Moselle river near Kobern while supporting the 87th Division's attack towards Koblenz on 16 March 1945. The tank crew has placed the fluorescent air identification panel on the turret roof.

A M4 tank of the 735th Tank Bn. is ferried across the Moselle river by engineers on 16 March 1945.

A M4A3 of the 784th Tank Bn. (Cld) provides fire support for the 104th [Divisi]on during fighting along the Rhine on 1 February 1945. This was one [of two] black tank battalions in the northwest Europe campaign in 1944-45.

A M4A3 (76) of the 784th Tank Bn. (Cld) during fighting along the Rhine in March 1945. This tank is fitted with metal chevron track and duck bill extenders.

A M4A3 (76) of the [784]th Tank Bn. (Cld) in [ope]rations near [Ha]slaken on 26 March [194]5 while supporting [the]35th Division.

The 157th Infantry Regt., 45th Div. began house-to-house fighting for Aschafenburg on 28 March, finally capturing the city on 3 April. During the final stage of the fighting, there was an encounter between a M36 tank destroyer of the 645th Tank Destroyer Bn. and this captured M4A3 (76) tank being used by the Germans. Besides the German crosses, the words "Beute panzer" (captured tank) were painted on the M4A3 (76) to prevent German troops from firing on it. It was knocked out by a 90mm hit on the glacis plate evident above the right headlight. (Patton Museum)

A column from the 9th Armored Division awaits orders in a farm field outside Westhousen, Germany on 10 April 1945. Behind and to the right of M4A3 is one of the new M32 armored recovery vehicles.

A M4A3 of Task Force Shaughnessy, CCR, 9th Armored Division covers the Mulde river bridge in Colditz, Germany 16 April 1945 shortly after the city was captured. operation was famous for the seizure of the Colditz fortress which was being used as a prisoner of war camp for 1, Allied soldiers.